LEARN THE PRINCIPLES OF ENTERING INTO GOD'S REST

YOU DON'T HAVE TO
BE DEAD
TO
REST
IN
PEACE

Apostle Sammy C. Smith

I0081186

Copyright ©2014 by Sammy C. Smith

Library of Congress Number: 2007012345

ISBN Number: 978-0-9832187-5-3

Published by Grace Us Living Publications (GULP)

Published in the United States of America

I have the deed to my own freedom.

Apostle Sammy C. Smith

This book is dedicated

To

YOU!

Continue to SEARCH for your PEACE...

ACKNOWLEDGEMENTS

To GOD,

ALL Glory to YOU, who has through Your mighty power at work within me, has accomplish infinitely more than I have ask or think. (Eph. 3:20)

Thank You!

To ALL my spiritual sons and daughters who worked on this project and labored in prayer... Thank You!

May God's Blessings continue to guide and follow your life!

Table of Contents

Introduction

As those connected to the Grace Cathedral Movement leave 2013, the year of "All or Nothing", God said, "Sammy, tell the people that I know the many struggles they have endured for the past seven years. They are still here and have endured the intensity of the attacks. They have persevered and endured like good soldiers. I have elevated them to another level." God said, "You have paid the price that has caused you to be victorious. The devil didn't kill you. *You Don't Have To Be Dead To Rest In Peace"!* He declares, "you shall live and not die and enjoy your life!" During your next seven years, you will discover God's peace and His rest; and see the manifestation of the blessings that you have believed Him for in your life.

It doesn't matter what you have been through, you must let go of the past and embrace the *rest* God has made available from the beginning of time. Often times our biggest problem is letting go of what was and embracing what is. That's what the people in the book of Hebrews were experiencing. They could not let go of the old and embrace Jesus Christ, The New. Therefore, they could not enter into the rest that God has made available for them.

God gave me this prophetic declaration to reassure His people, *"You Don't Have To Be Dead To Rest In Peace."* He wanted to assure them that they can live and have an abundant life, no matter what's going on around them. No, they don't have to live life any longer struggling, worried, stressed, depressed and sick, living in lack; nor wondering if God is going to do what He has promised. God has already made provisions for you. Stop wasting your time trying to make something happen. When you understand and believe God's Word, you can enter into that rest. His provision, purpose and peace were made available for you before the foundation of the world.

It is obvious we are living in a world of uncertainty and filled with insurmountable problems and issues. Many people pray to God, but they lack understanding of His Word. Therefore, they are not seeing the manifestation of His promises. Their lack of faith in God causes them to rely on the world's methods and solutions, *artificial intelligence.* The lack of knowing and understanding His Word keep them from receiving the purpose and provision God made for them from the foundation of the world. This is the main reason why many people rely and depend more on the medical world and prescription drugs to give them their answers. Ultimately, relief and healing can only come through God's Word. *"But he was wounded for our transgression, he was bruise for our iniquities: the chastisement of our peace was upon him; and with His stripes, we are healed."* (Isaiah 53:5)

God never promised His people they would not go through trials and tribulations. What He did promise was, *"Peace I leave with you, my peace I give unto you: not as the world give, give I unto you. Let not your heart be troubled, neither let it be afraid.* (John 14:27) He also assured them that they can endure like good soldiers! (2Timothy 2:3) What that means is, no matter what attack or problem we are faced with, we can overcome them. God's people can have the peace that brings freedom, while enjoying their lives.

As we explore Hebrews, we will discover that in order to enter into God's rest, we need to know and understand the true meaning of "His Rest." First of all, being spiritually mature to the point that our trust and faith in God is beyond what we can see. Secondly, we must be aware of what is keeping us from His rest. Finally, we must develop a hunger and a thirst to seek after His Kingdom or His ways of doing things.

"You Don't Have to be Dead to Rest in Peace" will help you in surrendering your will by not trusting ourselves and others; but instead, relying on the promises of God. You may ask yourself, "How do I place my full trust in God and His promises?" Understanding that our inability to enter God's rest on our own is the beginning of our freedom.

This book correlates the similarity of the first four chapters of Hebrews. Each paragraph take us on a journey into our lives to stretch our faith in understanding how to receive His peace. It is divided into three parts, the symptoms, the diagnosis and the cure. You will discover your rights and privileges during your transformation so that your audio will match your video. The journey will continue as it uncovers the controlling and manipulating effects of artificial intelligence which has made us robots, and many life changing principles that will change your life.

It is my prayer that God will give you the answers needed to receive and enter into His rest. *"So there is a special rest still waiting for the people of God. For all who have entered into God's rest have rested from their labors, just as God did after creating the world, so let us do our best to enter that rest. But if we disobeyed God, as the people of Israel did, we will fall."* (Hebrews 4:9-11)

Part One

The Symptoms

The Symptoms

How do we enjoy our life when we are being attacked with everyday problems and the unresolved issues? What do we do when our body gives us symptoms and it feels like our body is right? Regardless of what symptoms we are feeling or afflictions we are experiencing, we can be healed from everything and anything. It can be a broken heart, broken limb, a disease, or the paralyzing hand of death upon our body, ultimately, we are healed! Whether the symptoms is in the head, heart, or if it's an actual reality, GOD is the Great Physician. Healing belongs to every believer of Jesus Christ. It is the children's bread (Matthew 15:26). As a born again believer, His Word has the power to solve every problem or issue.

A symptom, according to Merriam Webster's dictionary, is a subjective evidence of disease or physical disturbance observed by the patient. It is something that indicates the presence of a physical disorder. The body's stress response kicks in when we are alarmed or threatened by anything. The heart beats faster, blood pressure spikes and we breathe faster. This means our heart pumps maximum oxygen and energy-rich blood to our muscles. The liver releases more glucose/energy into our blood to get it ready for action. The brain is the most complex organ in the human body; therefore, it is in super alert mode. It is made up of many specialized areas that work together. The cerebral cortex plays a key role in memory, attention, awareness, thought, language, perceptual and consciousness. This is the physical process of the body's symptoms, but God's Word acts as the solution by dissolving whatever feeling or symptoms when spoken over it.

When we speak God's promises, He rejects the symptoms, by faith. You may still feel the symptoms, but when we keep our mind on the promises and not on the symptoms, it will destroy the yoke and bondages. By faith means, things are not what they appear to be. His Word says the truth of the matter. You must know that according to Isaiah 53:5 and 1 Peter 2:24-b, God sees you as already healed. Jesus has already paid the price. You are healed, but it is Satan's job to try to kill you. Unless you know that as fact, he will deceive you into believing you are being destroyed by that lying symptom. The Word has permanence over the attention you give to the symptoms. Satan will use your mind and fill it with doubt and unbelief, by telling you that God's Word will not work for you. But that is a lie because God cannot lie! He will prove His Word if you dare to use His Word to decree it in the face of the enemy. Even with pain and symptoms, you must still confess God's promises. Therefore, speak His Word over all your symptoms without accepting the doctor's diagnosis. Don't ignore the doctor's prognosis, instead talk to and tell the diagnoses that it is illegally there and that you reject the diagnosis.

Ultimately, you are to declare God's promise over the doctor's diagnosis, instead of entertaining it. You have the right to decree the promises of God. Jesus paid the cost to redeem you from the curse of sickness by the stripes that He took upon His back. Proclaim God's promises, but don't claim it as a problem. Acknowledge it; for the sole purpose to use in spiritual warfare. You must know what is coming against your body in order to fight effectively in your spiritual battling! We often confess the condition, instead of saying what God's Word says over the condition. The condition may be a reality; but it isn't faith. Faith speaks what God says over conditions. Your faith along with God's Word cancels out any symptoms! (2 Corinthians 4:13)

Chapter One

The Last Seven Years

The declaration made on New Year's Eve 2013 Watch Night Service, over the people of God, was for the purpose of freeing them from the weariness and hopelessness. Their faithlessness had caused them to believe that God would not show up in making the provisions He had promised. The key in receiving any prophetic declaration is in the spiritual hearing of those who are listening. Therefore, *"He that hath an ear, let him hear what the Spirit saith unto the churches."* (Revelation 2:29)

God gave me a prophetic declaration for His people, but let's be clear of what means is. The true meaning of *prophetic declaration* is when God uses His Word to perform a thing. The power is in the word(s) being released, spoken or declared. It could bring death and life to what it's being spoken. (Proverbs 18:21). Prophesy brings to life anything that is wounded, dead or not functioning properly. Keep in mind, prophesy cannot manifest naturally until the process of spiritual maturity has been completed. What happens, God sends a prophetic declaration through a man or woman of God that He chooses. It usually is for the purpose of reassuring His people of their destiny. He knows that during times of hardship and struggle, people often get discouraged because their lives are bombarded with problems and unresolved issues. During those times, things do not appear to be in line with who they are and the purpose God has called and chosen for them. Actually, a believer's life should be one of speaking, confessing and declaring God's Word, no matter what is happening; they stay united and connected with the Word.

Declaration means to speak, declare, pronounce or to proclaim. God knew the people needed a powerful *Word* that would build, exhort and edify. He knew that the seven year journey had been rough and that many who began the journey had gotten weary in well-doing and had became discouraged. Secondly, He wanted those who were truly assigned to the movement to be encouraged. Thirdly, He wanted the people to know that He foreknew and allowed everything that occurred in their lives over the course of the past seven years; and was part of His plan. Finally, He also wanted those who had left their assignment, to return and complete it.

The primary reason God sends prophetic declarations is to encourage His people to stay on the spiritual path, so they can receive the blessings connected to their spiritual inheritance. In spite of everything that took place in the people lives, it was time for them to move out of their discouragement.

God's rest was waiting for them to enter, but they couldn't enter until they receive the peace of God, which comes only through spiritual transformation.

The book of Hebrews tells us that the Jews had been going through pure hell like many of us. It is not clear who the Hebrews writer is, but the style of writing is similar to the Apostle Paul's. He began his writing by making it clear that Jesus came to earth in the form of man in order that He could feel the pain of the people. He had to go through everything that man went through. *"For we have not an high priest which cannot be touched with the feeling of our infirmities; but was in all points tempted like as we are, yet without sin."* (Hebrews 4:15) We too must go through life's issues in order to get the experience needed to help others. It's the process of going through the pain from the experience that gives us the power to become powerful and life changing witnesses of Christ Jesus.

Unfortunately, the Jews in Hebrews had similar problems like we have today. They refused to let go of their old way of thinking. All they ever knew was Judaism and wanted to hold on to what they had been taught. In fact, like many of us today, their religion wasn't really producing the changes needed to make their lives better.. They were afraid that they would lose something if they gave it up. Fear was the source of the thought of their potential loss. Satan has convinced us too that we have to hold onto things we really don't need. They could not let go of the old, embrace Jesus Christ, and receive the peace and rest God made available to them. *'Isn't it something when God is trying to give us an upgrade and we refuse to download it?'*

Feelings of doubt, fear, and unbelief the Jews were experiencing, led them to many years of feeling rejected. Before Jesus came on the scene, God sent many prophets and teachers to reassure them that they were His sons; but the brutal effect of trauma from the emotional pain had engrained into negative feelings. They had been emotionally wounded, scarred and brainwashed by the system that had been downloaded in them. Their religious ideology kept them in spiritual bondage and their mind-set blocked them from receiving the new truth God was making available to them.

Rejection is one of the biggest negative seed that contributes to doubt, unbelief and fear. When God sent Jesus, the Jews rejected Him and had a hard time receiving the new truth. When we refuse to let go of religiosity or what they were taught in the past, God cannot do the downloading necessary to transform and renew our minds. Therefore, leaving us feeling like victims rather than more than conquerors. (Romans 8:37)

In order to let go of the past and receive the new

truth of God's Word, we must ask God to forgive, deliver, and develop us. Forgetting the things in our past that still dictate and dominate our decisions and actions are mostly the things we have been taught erroneously. It is hard to forget what has been familiar, but when we hold on, it won't bring fruit to our lives. Ultimately, the hell the people of the Grace Cathedral Movement had gone through or you had endured, the past seven years was God trying to kill some dead things from all of our lives. Our flesh is undisciplined and even though we are saved, our flesh is not. When we accepted Jesus, our spirit man was born again, but we must allow the process of our flesh to be crucified by spending time with God in His Word. The fruit of the spirit have to be developed.

There are nine fruit of the spirit. Galatians 5:22-23 teaches, "*But the Holy Spirit produces this kind of fruit in our lives, love, joy, peace, patience, kindness, goodness, faithfulness, gentleness and self-control. There is no law against these things.*" When we gave our hearts to Jesus and accepted Him, these fruit were seeded or planted in our spirit. The development of these fruit gives us the supernatural ability to experience the character of the fruit. A life of peace and joy is exhibited in any circumstance, no matter how painful and difficult it may be. Our developed fruit produce the ability to be more loving, patient, kind, peaceful, faithful, graceful, joyful, longsuffering, gentle, and more self controlled.

The Apostle Paul describes it by saying that we were controlled by our old sinful nature, but now we have been released when we became children of the most High God. We died and are no longer captive to its power. The development of our fruit frees us of the habits and desires that are not making our lives better. As we grow and develop, we can better control our unproductive thoughts, desires and actions. We react less negatively to behaviors that cause unfruitful actions that do not produce fruit in our lives. The fruit of the spirit help us to develop character and integrity that is needed to deal with people properly. We treat others better and become more loving and faithful servants of God. On our own, we don't have the ability and it would be impossible to overcome many of our negative behavior and actions. Ultimately, this supernatural ability helps us to love others and our neighbors. The truth is *'I can't love my neighbor, until I can see myself as my neighbor.'*

The term *"killing you"* actually means our process of sanctification. It simply means allowing God to take us on a journey of spiritual transformation that will produce growth and development in becoming spiritually mature. The transformation equips us to go to the next level or place that God could use us. All the problems and unresolved issues that we may have gone through is usually what He uses to kill the areas in our flesh that need to die. God knows that only radical people can tackle where God may be taking us to use us. He uses folks who have been drugged through the worse situations of life and have been counted out by others. God uses them because what they have experienced have also equipped them. The point is that God wants to get us to our spiritual place of having resurrection power. What that means is, He wants us to die in some areas which still have control over the old way of thinking and believing.

"Stay on Your Cross Until You Die!"

The resurrection power is designed to kill or get rid of those old thoughts and ideas of religiosity. The Bible says the letter kills. (2 Cor.3:6) The Word of God is supposed to kill; but the spirit of the Word is designed to kill us and give us new life. *'Isn't it something that the same thing that causes us to flourish, or to live, and not die, also kills'?* The concept of this term of "killing" means to allow the Word of God and the Holy Spirit to get rid of or annihilate old thoughts and produce behavior through reading, studying and understanding the Word of God. It means becoming transformed from our old way of thinking, renewing the mind, and guided into new truth. Actually the Word of God is the prescription that kills negative thoughts and actions that keep us from living a holistic and healthy life.

Unfortunately, instead of using God's Word to

lead, guide, and shape our lives, many of God's people use the Bible as an assault weapon to condemn, judge and kill others. When we apply or use it on ourselves, it should be used as our mirror. The purpose of God's Word is to give us a reflection of ourselves to show us how we look. It could bring revival to our soul and heal all heartaches, hurt or painful area in our lives. CAUTION! We must acknowledge what we see about ourselves and surrender it to God. This begins a resurrection process. *'When you are on your cross, your hands and feet are nailed to the cross. The only thing you can use is your mouth.'* Confession of God's Word while in the midst of pain, suffering or uncomfortable circumstances is the only weapon we should use as our weapon while being resurrected.

It's impossible to be resurrected before any burial. Everything about God's spiritual transformation is about death, burial and resurrection. That's God's system or His process. Many of us haven't died in some areas. That's why we can't be buried yet. When it isn't done in this order, we operate in a suspended arena. We are not effective and are unable to accomplish or get the things done needed to carry out and complete our assignment. We become discouraged, hopeless, doubtful and don't trust God. The reason is, we simply won't allow God to kill some fleshy areas of our lives by staying on our own cross and going through our very own resurrection. Jesus went through His resurrection. He suffered from hurt and pain. He hung on the Cross until He died. He was buried in a tomb. Finally, He was resurrected. Journeying through the entire process, He received the power to defeat sickness, pain and death itself. By going through the entire process, He has power, authority and dominion over any and all things to defeat and overcome them completely. We too must follow Jesus and His process for our personal spiritual resurrection. Shortcuts must be eliminated!

Clearly, we must understand, it's impossible to resurrect from hurt. We can only get resurrected from death. Our hurt has to be dead in order for us to be resurrected. We too have to die on the cross and be buried, before we can be resurrected. The same exact order applies to us. The same analogy goes with any hurt. I am reiterating the process again because we have to get this! The hurt and the pain have to hang on a cross until it dies or no longer exists! It must then be buried or put in the ground or tomb. There must be no life left; then we are resurrected. Only then do we have life. It's not until we complete this process that we can use the experience from it and bring life to others. Make no mistake; ALL flesh has to die completely. We cannot go into a comatose state or become unconscious. Those fleshy areas must die. We cannot be effective in our spiritual assignment until the process is FINISHED! After the resurrection, God is ready to download an upgrade inside us.

Upgrade, according to the Merriam-Webster Dictionary, is an area or surface that goes upward; an upward slope, or: an occurrence in which one thing is replaced by something better, newer, more valuable. We are talking about a spiritual upgrade in understanding the spiritually transformation what has taken place so we can move to the next spiritual place that God want us to be operating in. In most cases upgrades are free; we hesitate or simply don't take it. Remember, we must let go of everything that could hinder or stop us! Paul reminds us in Philippians 3:13, *"Brethren, I count not myself to have apprehended: but this one thing I do, forgetting those things which are behind, and reaching forth unto those things which are before."* He says, *"I press toward the mark for the prize of the high calling of God in Christ Jesus."*

What's ironic is we are now in a new place and a New Year when God gave the declaration to His people during the New Year's Watch Night Service. God sent His assurance of His promise to seal the deal. It is now time to receive the upgrade and enter into His rest. This is not just another book; its purpose is to sincerely help usher God's people into their spiritual place so they can receive this freedom that only come through spiritual understanding. Keep in mind that feelings of weariness are a part of the journey. When we become weary, discouraged and want to give up, DON"T GIVE UP! Read, study and meditate on Philippians 3:13. Keep pressing forward. God wants us to be encouraged; get alone with Him, read His Word, do what He says, so He can upgrade us to the next level in Him.

Can I Get A Witness?

God called us to be His witnesses. Therefore, He helps us to better understand spiritual revelations through everyday life occurrences. He does this so that we can testify, share and be a witness to others. What better way to help me understand "upgrade" than by dropping me in this real life encounter.

One day, I went to my phone carrier to get my upgrade. As the clerk was transferring the numbers from my old phone to the new, I started worrying about the possibility of him not transferring all the numbers. I was afraid that he would leave some of my old numbers in the old phone. I asked him, "Are you sure that you transferred all the numbers?" He assured me that he did. The clerk tried to alleviate my hesitation, and invited me to check for myself. As I was about to take the phone out of the clerk's hand, God said, "Sammy, sometimes it's good to get rid of some old stuff." God continued and said, "Sammy, there are some things in your life you need to erase."

God continued to deal with me, He said, "What's in your past that you want to hold onto? Is it possible, Sammy, that you may have hit the send button to your phone too quickly?" By this time, God really had me thinking. Before I could think any more about what He was saying, God continued speaking to me. God turned the conversation into another direction. It seemed God didn't want me to stay in His past conversations long, before He said, "But just like I erased everything on the phone with one press of a button, I'm God enough to throw your sins from the east to the east. I can erase everything that you have done in your past. I don't care who remembers. I will remember them no more." (Hebrews 8:12) *"What shall we then say to these things? If God be for us, who can be against us?"* (Romans 8:31)

I Think I Better Let It Go!

It's one thing when we hold ourselves hostage to our past, but it's another thing when others don't want us to forget. Unfortunately, there are some people who want us to stay in our old, depleted, defeated conditions and would like it if you never received an upgrade. There are some people who have negative feelings about your future. They don't ever want you to grow and live better lives. It doesn't matter what you do, there are people who will always criticize, backbite, and even discourage you to your face. It is important to realize some people are sent into your life to reject you. They were assigned to come into your life for that purpose. It often hurt, but it's really good for you. Their negative forces are building areas in you that need constructing. God allows us to go through rejections and negative reactions of people. He orders our footsteps into the paths of those who really don't know us or know how God sees us. They find it very inviting to bring back negative things about our life.

These are the challenges that make us great. If God can trust us around negativity and we still remain focused and positive, that is the greatest sign of growth. Some people conclude that you should only be around or surround yourself with people that celebrate you; that would defeat the purpose of development and expansion. We have to learn how to endure and get above negativity in the right spirit and watch God bring ultimate victory. Actually, we spend more time worrying about who don't like us or who talked about us, instead of paying attention to the more important things that should draw our attention.

Paying attention to the smallest details, (although they may not matter) is also important as we grow and develop spiritually. Often we think that minor things are less important, but the Holy Spirit is always changing. The Holy Spirit isn't religious or systematic. In Hebrews Chapter 2, the writer advises his listeners to pay attention to the new truth they had heard so that they wouldn't drift back into the old religious thoughts. Paying attention to the small detail of things is often hard. It involves keeping our minds and bodies focused. Staying focused does not mean simply listening, but also obeying. Paying attention can help you complete your assignments, no matter what it is.

When you pay attention to details you can see the entirety of any vision. As the Holy Spirit guides, it reveals the small, intricate details that naturally would be missed without the Holy Spirit shining some light on it. We become more strategic at planning and carrying out duties that are assigned. An individual who pays attention to detail have a low tolerance for routine tasks, but is excited and look forward to new and better ways of doing things. They are the ones that grab on to new and better concepts and understand spiritual and abstract principles.

More importantly, we must also pay attention to the spiritual meaning of the number seven. It is the number of completeness and perfection. All throughout bible history, from the seven days of Genesis to the Seven Seals of Revelation, the number seven have a spiritual and symbolic significance. God laid the foundation when He introduced it in the finish work of Creation. "*And on the seventh day, God endeth His work which He had made and rested on the 7th day from all His work he had made.*" (Genesis 2:2). It does not matter the pain and agony suffered in the last seven years, as long as we realize that it took seven years for God to complete the work needed. Forgiveness is one thing that could easily be hidden or forgotten. It is much needed so we ourselves could receive forgiveness from God and receive His blessings. Paying attention to and not forgetting to forgive those who may or may not contribute to some of our pain is very important. We say with our lips we forgive, but the unforgiveness remain hidden in our hearts. Jesus reminds us to forgive seventy times seven. In other words, He is telling us to keep on forgiving until we are complete. The fact that we have come out of the previous seven years means we are complete for where God is taking us. We are still alive and on the move for Christ. We can no longer hold any unforgiveness. In order to receive God's blessing, forgiveness is a must.

Isn't it amazing that our life operates in cycles of seven. According to scientific research, it takes seven years for our physical bodies to change. Most cells in our body are renewed over a seven year span. It's no wonder it took God seven years to do the work needed done to our hearts. I also read that according to the universal cosmic, the universe is form, exists and held together by seven principles. Cause and Effect is one. It is too much to go in details about the seven laws. That's another book. The bottom line is that the duration of the seven years and its experiences had an effect on everyone involved.

Everything happens according to a law. The trial, problems, issues and challenges we experienced the past seven years, means we had to overcome the lower laws before we could be exposed to the higher ones. It was the uncomfortable experiences that helped us to rise above them. It is a process. Therefore, our past experiences have elevated us to a new place that will expose us to higher laws. We must pay attention to the details so we don't miss is because that's part of the process of entering into His Rest!

Chapter Two

Memory vs. Imagination

In the book of Hebrews, the Jews' memory kept them from seeing the vision that God was trying to download into them. Their inability to completely surrender what they had learned blinded them. If they simply could let go of their previous download, they could begin to create and imagine. Instead, their memory had more power over them than their imagination. All throughout history, God sent apostles, prophets, women and men of God to assist in the upgrading of the people's imagination. They refused the upgrade and remained stuck in their old "stinking thinking." People hate changes!

'We always shout about God's unchanging hand, but we can't see God's unfolding hands.'

When we begin to see God's unfolding hands, we would be able to forget the past and see where God is headed. God's unfolding hand is so powerful. In His unfolding hand, we can see vision. The Bible says, *"Where there is no vision, the people perish"* (Proverbs 29:18). What that really means is, where there is no revelation, there will soon be extinction. To illustrate, let's take a look at what God is unfolding in ministries all over the world. Many churches are shutting down and closing their doors. Many of them have lost their grip and vision. God unfolds vision by constantly changing things, so we don't get stuck on memory nor on what was or what could have been. He unfolds to stir up our imagination in creating more new and life changing ways of presenting the Gospel to the world.

God's Intelligence System (GI)

During creation, when God spoke man into existence, He was actually saying, *'Let ME make man so He can imagine like ME and do like I say.'* God is so creative that He had a variety of form and shapes for man. He formed each of us unique for the sole purpose of thinking and creating like Him. When God made man, He placed a spiritual and intelligence system in him during Creation that gives us the stamina and endurance to withstand everything. God's intelligence (GI) System is His Word. When we read, study and understand God's Intelligence (GI) System, we gain the ability to recreate from what He created in the beginning of time. We have His DNA, therefore, we have the fortitude to think and imagine the answer to every problem and issues in the world. Becoming creative often mean doing things over and over again.

Repetition is the force needed to get His Word

downloaded in our spirit. The consistency of anything usually bring forth great results, but hearing and reading His Word equips and prepares us to combat the world's system or the Artificial Intelligence (AI) that has invaded and programmed the minds of God's people. The Bible tells us that, *"All scripture is given by inspiration of God, and is profitable for doctrine, for reproof, for correction, for instruction in righteousness: That the man of God may be perfect, thoroughly: furnished unto all good works."* (2 Timothy 3:16-17) We must hear and confess the Word over and over again! "Faith comes by hearing over and over again." (Paraphrased) (Romans 10:7)

The Word is a continual reminder of the power God placed in us. It is alive and full of power, making it active, operative, energizing and effective. It is sharper than any two-edged sword, penetrating to the dividing line of the breath of life (soul) and (immortal) spirit and of joints and marrow into the deepest parts of our nature, exposing (AI) and sifting (AI), analyzing (AI), judging the very thoughts and purpose of the heart (AI). (Hebrews 4:12) Therefore, God's people have their own GI system downloaded and do not have to rely on the world's AI system.

Artificial Intelligence (AI)

Paul dares us to be different. He warns us to be

radically different from others in the world. He reminds us *"Do not conform to the pattern of this world, but be transformed by the renewing of your mind.* (Romans 12:2-3) God through Moses, told the Israelites, *"You must not do as they do in Egypt, where you used to live, and you must not do as they do in the land of Canaan, where I am bringing you. Do not follow their practices. You must obey my laws and be careful to follow my decrees. I am the Lord your God."*(Leviticus 18:3-4)

It is time for the people of God to no longer allow the AI that has been downloaded from previous generations to continue to dictate to them. Artificial Intelligence (AI), according to Merriam Webster is the theory and an area of computer science that deals with giving machines the ability to seem like they have human intelligence. This includes traits such as visual perception, speech recognition, decision-making, and translation between languages. In other words, we have been programmed as to how and what we see, say, believe and rely on the systems of this world to influence and dictate to us what is best for our life.

AI will never be able to compare to the power of God and His systems and ways. Jesus told His disciples, *"do not be like them."* (Matthew 6:8) God repeatedly warns against the AI's of this world, but what do many believers do? They fail to equip themselves with the GI system and fall prey to AI. GI

System is the Word of God! Without GI System, it's easy to fall into the hands of AI. It's cunning, seducing and manipulating. It looks inviting, convenient and lures the vulnerable right into it. Its strategy is to find out where and what we lack and it gives us just enough bait to convince and gain our loyalty. Therefore, we become dependent on it, leaving us in a desperate state. It programs humans to think the way it wants them to think in order to gain control of the minds of the vulnerable.

The Bible reminds us that though we live in this world, we are not of this world. (John 15:17-19) God blesses us by providing new and better conveniences to enjoy, not allowing anything to have control over our lives. God wants us to enjoy His blessings in moderation. He expects us to have balance in our lives. First Peter 5:8 talks about *being well-balanced because our adversary, the devil, our enemy, is seeking (looking for areas that lack God's Word) to cause harm.* If we would think for a moment, the areas in our lives where we are undisciplined and is the least balanced, is an area that Satan uses to steal, kill and destroy. Physical and spiritual abuse is the reason why many people suffer from relational hurt, illness, sickness and disease, lack and poverty. When we put our trust in any other person or system other than God, we fall into Satan's grip. Under no circumstances are we to ever believe there is a comparison to God's message and the GI System.

The manipulating and controlling power of AI has invaded vast portions of our communities. Actually, AI is not prejudice. It uses its manipulating power, regardless of race, creed, color, class or gender! People are hurting and are more dependent on doctors, prescriptions, and the medical world to null their pain. Instead, they have become dependent, despondent and depleted by them. Many are ignorant to the fact that the world is spending billions of dollars on medication simply to prolong their lives, but never being cured; all while these billion dollar industries are getting richer and acquiring more wealth. Yet, many people are walking around like zombies barely existing. They are like robots because the AI of this world has programmed them to believe in a god, other than the true and living God.

No Information – No Revelation

We live in a world where information can be easily obtained through many different sources or vehicles: reading, listening and watching DVD's, CD's, cell phones, iPads, laptops, computers and many more vehicles God has made available for us to acquire information. Reading and studying God's Word is the primary source in building our spiritual foundation and knowledge of God's ways of doing things.

(Matthew 6:33)

Reading from a wide assortment of resources is vitally necessary to facilitate attaining knowledge. When we read and listen to various books, publications, music and movies, it broadens our way of thinking and gives the Holy Spirit tools to revolutionize our minds. The Bible says, *"See then that ye walk circumspectly, not as fools, but as wise, redeeming the time, because the days are evil."* (Ephesians 5:15-16)

It is important to walk circumspectly in the world. We should be spiritually equipped to move under the leading and power of the Holy Spirit. We redeem the time we spend on this earth when we try to live as vessels of honor. Though we live in the world, our lives ought not to be in any way, shape or form, like that of the world. The more information we read or learn, the more the Holy Spirit has to work with in revealing new and better things to us. Acquiring information teaches us to live more cautiously, wiser and morally. God's people's lives should be one of simplicity, thankfulness, soberness, faithfulness, and full of praiseworthiness. Walking circumspectly can make such an impact to an unbelieving world of our commitment to fulfill God's purpose for our lives.

We recognize God in what we read in the world today. It makes us wise and helps us to abstain from the evil that plagues our nation and the world. The Bible reminds us, *"Grace be to you and peace from God the Father, and from our Lord Jesus Christ, Who gave himself for our sins, that he might deliver us from this present evil world, according to the will of God and our Father.* (Galatians1:3-4) More importantly, it is impossible to walk circumspectly without reading and studying God's Word, Seeking His will for our lives is key to knowing what's going on around us. Reading allows us to acquire knowledge. Knowledge is power. It is equally important that we understand the more we learn and read, the more God will reveal to His people!

Unfortunately, many of God's people do not read nor do they understand. They are unaware of what is going on right in their own neighborhood and community. Many in the Body of Christ are ignorant to God's Word and this is the entrance Satan uses to attack us. The more we know, the more we grow.

Lack of Understanding

Understanding is the key that unlocks the door to every resource in life. We are reminded in Proverbs 4:7, *"Wisdom is the principal thing; therefore get wisdom: and with all thy getting get understanding."* More importantly, understanding the totality of the concept in Hebrews, chapter one through four is vital for entering God's rest. First of all, we enter God's rest by understanding that we do not have the ability to enter His rest in our strength. Why did God rest on the seventh day? In Genesis 2:2 we read, *"And on the seventh day God ended his work which he had made; and he rested on the seventh day from all his work which he had made."* You may ask, "If God is omnipotent, if He has all power, it doesn't make sense that He would need to 'rest.' He rested on the 7th day as a symbol for man to take a physical day of rest. It doesn't say God "needed to rest"; it simply says He did. Also, the Scriptures are very clear that God did not rest because He was tired.

The Hebrew word translated "rested" in Genesis 2:2 includes other connotations than that of being tired. In fact, one of the main definitions of the Hebrew word Shabbat is "ceasing or stopping". In Genesis 2:2 the understanding is that God "stopped" His work. He "ceased" creating on the seventh day. All that He had created was good and His work was "finished." Hebrews chapters three and four tell us how to enter into God's rest. The meaning of "rest" in chapter three makes reference to the children of Israel wandering in the desert.

We must understand that when God gave them the land of Canaan, His promise to them was that He would go ahead of them, conquer and defeat all their enemies so they could live safe and secure. (Deuteronomy 12:9-10) The only thing God wanted from them was to believe, trust and obey Him and His promises. However, they refused! Instead, they whined and complained about Him. They were never satisfied and wanted everything when they wanted it. They didn't understand what God was doing and even whined to return back to Egypt and to their bondage (Exodus 16:3, Numbers 20:3-13). Doesn't that sound like us today? Our lacks of understanding cause us to whine and complain at the least little sign of discomfort or trouble. Our lack of understanding always causes us to be ungrateful and disobedient. We look for and accept solutions from every other source, except God.

His Rest

The meaning of "rest" referred to in Hebrews was the land of Canaan. God promised, the Israelites who rebelled and disobeyed Him, would never enter Canaan (Hebrews 3:11). God attempted so many times to reclaim them, but His efforts failed. He gave them chance after chance. God's tried to warn, entreat them; to cause His mercies to pass before them and visit them with judgment was all in vain. God then declared because of all their rebellion, they would be excluded from the Promised Land (Hebrews 3:16-19). Eventually, the next generation did place their faith in God. Forty years later, they entered into God's rest (spiritual), the land of Canaan (physical), as a result of following Joshua's leadership. (Joshua 3:14-17)

The Israelites are a good example of our disobedience today. We disobey God and expect God to always come to our rescue. God allows us to endure attacks, trials, and tribulations so that we can finally come to the realization that we need God and His way of doing things. *"Therefore, since the promise of entering his rest still stands, let us be careful that none of you be found to have fallen short of it"*. (Hebrews 4:1) The promise that still stands is the promise of salvation through God's provision, Jesus Christ. He alone can provide the eternal rest of salvation through His blood which was shed on the Cross for the remission of sins. God's rest then, is in the spiritual realm, the rest of salvation.

The Death Threat – The Enemy

Once we accept Jesus as our Savior, Satan becomes our enemy and we become his target. He is assigned to every believer's trail, and his primary goal is to steal, kill, and destroy all who belong to and are a part of God's family (John 10:10). He uses many tactics and strategies to attempt to bring us to our knees, defeat, and eventually destroy us. His strategy is to wage war on us by planting negative thoughts in our ears to cause doubt and fear. His entrance is usually what we see and hear.

Satan's main objective is to plant doubt and unbelief in the heart of the believer. What's ironic is that we use our words to say we believe God's Word, have gone to church most of our lives, and have heard all of the promises that God has made available for us through His Son, Jesus Christ. If the truth be told, many in the Body of Christ don't actually believe. That is one main reason why the hit man, Satan, has the power to continue to set up booby traps to ensnare us, make us miserable, and eventually destroys lives of the believer. The bottom line is Satan is aware of the rest God made available for us from the beginning of time and he does not want us to receive it. He continues to fight and torture the people of God. His goal is to keep us from a lifestyle of living in peace and abundance. He does not want us to enjoy our lives. Many may ask, "How does Satan know?" He is well aware of God's Word and His promises for His children, and he sees us fearful and not enjoying the life God intends for His children.

Satan wants us to remain ignorant by planting things in our ears that appear real. He knows how much God loves each and every one of His children. He is jealous of us because of that Truth. Satan realizes due to his disobedience and rebellion against God, he was kicked out of Heaven and can never return. Satan hates us because we have received the promises that he forfeited through his rebellion. He tries to sabotage every one of our promises. We must make a conscious decision to become aware of the tactics and schemes of the enemy to destroy every believer of Jesus Christ. Believers must know enough of God's Word to counterattack Satan and his strategies. Many of God's people are unskilled in spiritual warfare because we simply fail to study the Word of God and fail to communicate with God in prayer. Reading and studying God's Word equips us to become skilled in our counterattack with Satan.

We can be victorious in our battle by confessing the Word of God over whatever area the attack is concerning. When we are unskilled in spiritual warfare, we become fearful as we experience the different problems and issues of life. Rather than fighting spiritually, we are fearful and begin to waver and doubt. The reason we fear is simply because we don't have enough of God's Word in us. Instead, our mind convinces the body to respond and begin to give off signs and symptoms that we are stressed, sick and could possibly die. We then go to the hospital emergency room or doctor in search of answers to solve our health issues.

There are four things we need to be aware of. First, Satan hates us and is our enemy. Second, he will use anyone or any negative situation to deposit the seed of death. Third, he can and will use a person who we don't consider to be our enemy. Fourth, his strategy is simply to deposit the seed of death in our mind. He knows that the mind is the battlefield.

A personal witness to the assault example of Satan and how he attacks our mind is, one evening on my way to Bible Study, the funniest thing happened. I received a phone call from a number I didn't recognize. I knew it was a phone number from Sumter SC, the city where I planted my first church. When I answered the phone, the voice on the other end was that of a young man whose voice I immediately recognized. He began his conversation: *"Oh I guess the rumor that's out is not true about you being deceased?"* The bottom line was he called himself playing a joke. The only thing I found funny about it was the person playing the joke was an undertaker. My first thought was, if he only knew everything I had to endure, have been through and overcame, he wouldn't find his little prank funny. The realty of his joke was the undertaker probably was clueless that Satan was actually using him and his phone call to plant a seed of death on my life. This is simply confirming that Satan will use a person(s) who we least expect and he uses the ear to deposit the seed of death in our lives.

I Shall Live and Not Die

The fact of the matter is God has assignments for our lives. The enemy would love to plant thoughts that are negative and deadly in our ear and mind because of where we are going and the work we have to do for God. Remember, its Satan's job to steal, kill, and destroy us. Never be caught off guard by whom he uses to do the seed planting. He uses people who we least expect that could or would plant the seed of death. He will use a phone call as the gateway to our minds to deposit the negative seed. His mission is to convince us that we are not who God says we are.

Understand, our survival lies in first identifying who the enemy is and recognizing his tactics and the strategies he uses to keep God's people in a crippled state or condition. Never simply allow our emotions to cause us to give in to Satan's devices. Keep on declaring! God's people are chosen; as believers make the choice not to settle for anything that Satan throws our way. Fight back! Declare, 'I am not done! I choose not to die.' *"I shall not die, but live, and declare the works of the LORD."* (Psalm 118:17)

Part Two

The Diagnosis

The Diagnosis

A diagnosis is described as a procedure or test which is performed to determine what is wrong with a patient or identify a disease from its signs and symptoms. Some studies show that stress causes symptoms and requires a diagnosis and risk factor treatment. Stress is the body's reaction to everyday tension and pressure. Stress can also increase pain levels, dependent upon medical history.

The people in Hebrews were stressed because they refused to let go of religion and embrace the new life transformation that only Christ can bring. They could not accept and believe they could not find anything better than Christ. Instead of relying on Him, they relied on what they had learned previously. It was difficult for them to let go of the past and embrace the future. They could not put their trust in having Christ as the best, new thing in their lives. By holding onto their old religion, they couldn't see the deception and its cheap imitation that it brought. Therefore, they allowed the familiar to dictate, diagnose and control them. They looked for answers, cures, and remedies to their problems; but failed to understand their answer was right under their nose.

When we lack the understanding of God's Word, we lack the ability to embrace His peace and enter into His rest. It's impossible to do. One of the signs of worry and stress is lack of proper sleep and rest, which negatively affects our bodies. The signals lead us in search of answers or being diagnosed. At this stage, we often don't realize that God's Word gives us the diagnosis for anything that goes on with us. We think we need someone or something that is visible, to diagnose or tell us what's wrong, instead of going to the ONE who created and designed us. When we don't read or know what the Word of God says, the AI of this world has us programmed into its' system.

Every medical story begins with the body giving off symptoms and we run to the doctors for a diagnosis. Ironically, it's the "diagnosis" that rakes in the billions of dollars in medicine. Each symptom given by the patient is given a diagnosis code. The diagnosis code determines the cost of each service provided by the medical facility or physician. In other words, the diagnosis is what's making the money! The more symptoms you have, the more diagnoses are received, which results in more money being made. The lack of having Word in us causes us to think that the doctor writing the prescription or administering the drug, for the diagnosis is the cure and not God.

Chapter Three

What's Killing You?

So what's really killing us are the stresses of life and the manner in which we deal with them. It is common for a doctor to prescribe drugs for most common illnesses. Research shows that some prescribed drugs used to manage chronic pain tend to have unwanted side effects. One side effect is that the body has become used to the drug (developed a tolerance) and it has less effect on the body at a certain dosage. Another contributing factor is the powerful influence prescribed drugs have over many people, so they become dependent on them and have much faith in them.

Some of these commonly used drugs have the addictive power as the street drugs we have always been told to stay away from because they are deadly. We have seen the evidence of the power that some street drugs had on either ourselves or a loved one. These drugs control and manipulate through its drawing power to bait, persuade and deceive. Their seducing powers draw us in and make us feel good initially, while controlling and paralyzing the mind, destroying the bodily functions, and simultaneously depleting our money and resources.

While the FDA has deemed statins to be safe to use for their intended purpose, no drug is without side effects in susceptible individuals. The drug companies that manufacture statins have added a warning to the medicines' advertising and labels that was not present in previous ads. The warning tells patients about the possibility of muscle pain and weakness as a rare but serious side effect. Muscle pain and muscle weakness are two of the main side effects of statin drugs. The scientists who study this put them in a category called muscle-related adverse effects (MAEs). Another common side effect is memory loss. Anyone who is taking statin drugs for any reason should be aware of these side effects and their symptoms.

Researching and evaluating the medication prescribed for us is vital. No, we are not saying stop taking your medicine, or that all medicine is bad for us. The Word of God reminds us that "*All things are lawful unto me, but all things are not expedient.*" (1 Corinthians 6:12) Like anything, some good could be in medication. Actually, our spiritual belief and faith in God's Word is the key factor in our health and healing. We are not questioning the medical treatment and advice our doctor or healthcare professional is providing us. What we are saying, as people of God, we need to take control of our health, wellness, pain, and our lives.

God never intended for us to put our trust in man. He will use a man as a vessel, but has provided us with a guide, which is the Word of God and the Holy Spirit which lead and guide us into all truth. We must develop a wellness plan and be responsible for our own health by being proactive. In chapter two, we talked about AI and how it has conditioned our minds like robots. We are convinced into believing and relying on the idea that what the doctor prescribes is the answer to our health issues. God has made available many channels of resources so that we can investigate and become knowledgeable about all things. This is also true pertaining to our health and what is the best solution for us. Whose report are we going to believe? How can we believe that which we don't know? The Bible clearly reminds us that in ALL things we must understand (Proverbs 4:1-7). We can't understand what we simply don't know!

Faith Without Works Is Dead

Maintaining and adjusting our lifestyle does play a major role in our lifespan; but God has the ultimate plan for our health and our lives. We do what we can in taking care of our body. He gave us His faith to live by. The Bible declares that *"the just shall live by faith"* (Hebrews 10:38) and *'we are healed by our faith.'* Trusting God and His way of healing our bodies, will take our faith to another level. The Word of God is powerful. Believing God's Word brings healing. Trusting Him is also powerful. Will we believe God's Word or the word of the world's system? What do you believe is killing you? Whose report will you believe? (Isaiah 53:1-5)

All our lives we have allowed the world to reduce our restraint. Our resistance has been so depleted, that at the first sign of pain, we go to someone who we believe is capable of helping us. Do we understand that a healthy lifestyle determines our life expectancy? Life expectancy and lifestyle plays a major role in our lifespan. What we believe is powerful. There are so many things happening in the atmosphere that could be epidemic. What Hebrews teaches will build up our immune system. Making a conscious decision that Satan will no longer rob us of our thoughts and of the peace that God has made available for us is vital to our health, life expectancy, lifestyle and lifespan.

Chapter Four

Re-Present to Represent as (Sons)

Our spiritual growth and development is the prerequisite in becoming God's representation, or His son. First of all, understand that when we speak of "sons", this does not refer to gender. In order to represent or be a son of God, we must be on a spiritual journey to mirror Him or become like Him. One foundational problem is that many believers have been taught Scriptures erroneously. Therefore, one has the wrong perception of what it takes to represent our Lord and Savior Jesus Christ properly.

There are many in the Body of Christ that love and have been faithful to God; but unfortunately, are not seeing the blessings God has promised in their lives. It's so sad that many of God's people don't really see themselves as sons of God because they simply don't know their spiritual heritage. They don't believe who they are, because they don't know their true worth and value. They doubt their qualification as a son. How can we represent what we don't know?

We need to re-evaluate ourselves, take an honest inventory of where we are in our spiritual journey and allow God to take us through the process of being re-presented into becoming true sons of God.

Re-presenting is allowing the Holy Spirit to put a mirror in front of us and show us what is there and being honest about what the mirror reveals. It means we will surrender our will and allow God's Word to spiritually transform us into the image of God.

From the beginning of time God had a special purpose for man, "*And God said, Let us make man in our image, after our likeness: and let them have dominion over the fish of the sea, and over the fowl of the air, and over the cattle, and over all the earth, and over every creeping thing that creepeth upon the earth.*"(Genesis 1:26) God created man in His image and likeness and gave him authority to rule over all the Earth. God placed man and woman in the Garden of Eden in order to represent God's purposes and rule over all living things. All of creation saw something unique and glorious as they gazed upon Adam and Eve. This was God's purpose for Adam: to walk in the likeness of God, therefore reflecting the image of God, representing Him with authority and ruling the earth.

Men and women who represent God have solutions to the many problems that plague our world. We must represent like the power and strength of the Ark of the Covenant. The Ark carried the Word of God in it; because it had the Word and productivity in it (Numbers 17:6-8). When we don't read, study and believe the Word, it's impossible to carry the Ark. The same ingredient is required of a son; we must have productivity in us, just like the Ark of the Covenant. Ultimately, in order for sons to represent like God has designed and created us to, sons must carry something great. We must carry the weight of distributing whatever solution or healing is needed. When a son shows up, his spiritual weight and influence should be something so powerful that when he speaks, it brings hope and life back to whoever is listening and whatever is broken. Realistically, many folks don't meet the requirement simply because many have become too anxious and are spiritually immature. They don't have enough Word in them, yet want to operate in a capacity they are not prepared for. The sad reality is many leave tutelage too early and go out into the world and operate in a role of spiritual leadership, in which they are not equipped.

Many sons are out in the world wounded and because of their spiritual infection, they preach and teach messages from their hurt which are wounding and infecting those they come in contact with. What's sad is they think they are ready. Like a baby eagle, they leave the nest and fly out as though they can handle it; thinking they are mature. Sadly, many will find out they were not ready. Like the prodigal son, the father will allow them to go and still encourage them to "make it work".

Sons must represent properly in order to be

available for God's people. The Tabernacle was constructed for the purpose that the LORD would be among His people, also. *"And let them make me a sanctuary; that I may dwell among them."* (Exodus 25:8) In Jeremiah, they no longer needed the Ark of the Covenant. The Ark of the Covenant disappeared off the pages of history by the time of the Babylonian Captivity. There are many speculations about what happened to it. According to scripture, the last time The Ark was seen was in the eighteenth year of King Josiah's reign. He ordered the Ark of the Covenant to be returned to the temple of Jerusalem (2 Chronicles 35:1-6)

Overall, in order for the sons of God to represent God properly, they must represent like the Ark of the Covenant. They must go through a process of spiritual surrendering and maturity. The Ark was the place of the Lord's presence and its' purpose was to bring great assurance to the people of God. A son must develop this spiritual assurance. He must have resistance. God's assurance transfers to His sons. In other words, his video must match his audio.

Your Video Must Match Your Audio

When sons mature, their video matches their audio. They must know and carry the Word in their heart. A display a confidence and assurance is seen that will give off a radiance that will eventually transfer to the people they serve. In other words, they must become what and who we say we are. They must not only talk the talk, they must walk the walk. This means that they must grow up from being a whiner and complainer. They must become developed and matured into an overcomer.

The book of Exodus compares sons today to those in the Old Testament by saying, *"This high, lofty, majestic, and King dwelt among His grumbling, complaining, bickering, and sinful people."*(Exodus 15:24) Does that sound familiar? A spiritually mature son is humble, even when things may not be the way he wants. Instead of grumbling, complaining and bickering, they are consistent, faithful and walking in obedience to God. When sons operate in this capacity, we are thankful that God can handle whatever we may go through. We don't panic at the sign of trouble, but they rest in God, assured that He is not off in another land but always near.

The Sabbath rest mentioned in Hebrews Four is the promise of God's rest, but the peace lies in knowing that the Lord is near to us by the power of the Holy Spirit (1 Corinthians 6:19). It is the same in John 14:16 where Jesus promises His helpful presence. The assurance that His nearness brings was described by the Prophet Isaiah. sons of God should have enough Word in them to heal a hurting and dying world. The presence of God that sons possess has productivity in it. They can produce and conquer any challenge.

Finally, sons of God always evaluate their productivity. Am I producing? What am I producing? Am I making a difference? Even when sons of God look at themselves and find they are not producing or distributing anything, they have the courage to recognize, admit and communicate it to God. This is a component to entering the peace and rest of God that is available for each son of God. Sons become problem solvers and solution makers. We are mature sons of God when our video matches our audio. We have gone through the spiritual process of endurance.

Endurance Produces Assurance

When facing hardship, we often get discouraged and question our strength. We may even convince ourselves, "I just can't hold out." We question our ability to continue under whatever the circumstance may be and feel it would be impossible! We confuse this feeling to justify disobeying God. Rather, considering the promises of God that remind us that we can endure. We are tough! God will not allow us to face a temptation that is beyond our ability to endure (Matthew 24:13). Our assurance lies in knowing that for every temptation, God is our salvation.

This means we can endure every trial without deliberately sinning. If we think we "can't do' what

God said to do, or if we ever justify disobeying God, we have believed the Devil's lie. What we need to do is to quit looking for excuses and look instead, forward to our trial! Enduring means to outlast and go through the process and come out victorious. *"Many are the afflictions of the righteous; but the Lord delivers him out of them all."* (Psalm 34:19) God will, by no means, remove all our afflictions; He knows we have the ability to endure them. This endurance produces assurance when we arrive at the spiritual place of knowing that, *"no temptation or trial can separate us from God."* (Romans 8:35-39) Through and in all problems, we are "more than conquerors". We are more than conquerors because problems can actually make us better people. (Proverbs 24:10).

Problems Produce Solutions

Every struggle, problem and unresolved issue, prepares us for becoming solution makers to many of the problems the world faces. God has equipped us to conquer every problem He allows us to go through. We will always experience attacks, trials, troubles and problems. The Bible tells us, *"Man who is born of a woman is of few days and full of trouble."* (Job 14:1) We can be encouraged by these words when we think of the suffering endured by Job. We all deal with different problems and unresolved issues, but how do we handle them and come out of them?

Why do people suffer? Can problems and suffering actually help us become solution makers? We all face problems, affliction, suffering, and hardship. Sometimes we do question God. Scripture reminds us *"It is good for me that I have been afflicted."* (Psalm 119:71) When we suffer we can only see the problems involved; but if we remain faithful, spiritual growth happens. First Peter 1:6-7 confirms this by stating: *"So that (the genuineness) of your faith may be tested, (your faith) which is infinitely more precious than the perishable gold which is tested and purified by fire.* There are many reasons why people suffer, but it is quite clear that every person deals with problems differently. James 1:2 says we profit from trials, and we should count it all joy when trials come because trials are a testing of our faith. Our connections in Christ will cause every believer to conquer and be victorious in every situation.

Problems defeat some people, but strengthen others. Everyone experience problems. If problems and suffering were limited to sinners and believers never suffered, everyone would become believers in Christ; not because they really loved God, but just to avoid problems and suffering. Burdens can bring suffering and hardship which can lead us to spiritual temptation, as well as causing us to doubt God. We often become discouraged, tempted and feel our problems justify us relying on others who we feel may have the answers for our problems.

There are various reasons for trials and sufferings. Paul's "thorn in the flesh" was a messenger from Satan, yet God allowed it to remain because it kept Paul from becoming too proud over the many revelations he had received. (2 Corinthians 12:7-10) Through problems and suffering, God can produce great strength. Sons' tests and trials qualify them to be a great representation of God. It seems some folks suffer more hardships than others. We all know from personal experience and from the experiences of those we know, what Job says is true.

Many of God's people erroneously believe that jumping and shouting is all that is required to be victorious. Ignorance of the devil's devices is why so many are not seeing the blessings that we have inherited as believers. The Bible reminds us that God's people suffer because of lack knowledge and understanding. It's killing us. It's when we go through the process of any sickness or trial that our faith gets developed and we get first-hand experience of God's power. God is so pleased by the believer who, no matter what they go through, continues to bounce back. Our very own experience, gives us our own testimony. We have personal experience because we have been there. We become experts and our faith has increased to the point that in our mind, we understand and know that God can. We are in a "God can" state. We have confidence and assurance that God can bring us through anything.

Can I Get A Witness

Let's use a pilot as an example. If he is put in a cockpit and has never flown before, there could be a problem. On the other hand, if he has flown before, it's unlikely he will encounter any problems because he is an experienced pilot. He has become an expert and is the solution in flying a plane and getting the passengers to their destination safely. Another example is when a person can't swim and thrown in 20 feet of water. It's a problem to someone who can't swim; but if they can swim, that's not a problem. They will live and not drown.

Problems concern us, not just because suffering and hardship are burdens. Problems give us the experience needed to become experts. God intend for us to take the lessons learned from our negative experiences, grab a hold of the principles. Applying the principles could improve our lives and the lives of others. We live in a world where everyone has troubles and need our help.

Conversation and Meditation

Our communication with God does not develop with God through just church attendance. Having our own personal time in conversation and meditation develops a close and intimate relationship with God. Personal conversations and meditation helps us get through the tough times in life. Reading and meditation on God's Word is like that between a father and child. The irony is, we don't converse with Him, until we are going through some tough times and our back is up against a wall. When we've tried everything else, we are forced to seek God.

When we are bombarded with problems and unresolved issues, we can find peace in spending personal time with our Loving Father. When we live a lifestyle where our conversation with God is open, we are able to rely on receiving the answers and solutions to any problems we may encounter. Though we shouldn't wait for the difficult times to seek God, trials and problems are the draw that usually provokes us into talking to Him. It is during difficult times that we look for answers and relief to what seems too hard to bear.

Depending on the problem or season that we are experiencing, communing with God could be through Bible reading, conversation, meditation, or simply thinking through the Word of God. The way an individual chooses to converse with God is between them and God. The method used when spending time communing with God, often depends on where we are spiritually. Depending on the time and season of our life, or what we are dealing with, our patterns change. As we mature, we can discern what, how and when. Mature saints are led by the Spirit through how they communicate with Him.

Our communication with God should not be solely for the purpose of receiving stuff from God. It is during our private encounters with Him that He can reveal some of the not so lovely things about us. God covers our nasty stuff and won't expose the unattractive areas of our lives to those who don't love us. It is when we are alone with Him that He reveals or pulls back the covers and exposes the areas He need us to deal with.

The more frequent our conversation with God becomes, the more our meditation develops. Meditation is when we enter an intimate place with Him where we don't have to use His Word, nor our words audibly to communicate with Him. We now can "think" or meditate on Him. In conversation and meditation, we can talk or communicate with others, while still communicating with God. The more our desire increases in spending personal time in communication with God, the more He fills us with peace, rest and contentment during the most difficult times in our lives.

Content/Contentment

Contentment is a state of satisfaction that is anchored to our confidence in God that results in a joyful celebration of life. It's when we are grateful for whatever we are blessed with at that present moment and time. Everything in life is a process and we must go through the process to get to the expected end or desired result. Being content is containing the power of overcoming any problems, issues, sickness or disease. It's when we trust God in the situation at hand. The lack of trust in God's promises produced the lack of contentment. The Hebrews lack of contentment was brought about by their lack of trust and faith. Paul rejoices in Philippians 4:10 knowing that he has learned to be content in whatever circumstances he found himself in. When you think about the word 'circumstance,' it could mean 'a circle that you can stand!'

Contentment is a great virtue to have, but it is a learned state that you grow into over time. It is when we rely on God's sufficiency. Reaching this state of spiritual maturity does not come naturally. With our old human (fleshy) nature, we were created to always want more than we need, compare ourselves to others and to complain. What's ironic is that we were not taught any of these behaviors, yet we were born with these characteristics. It is not about what we own, it's about accepting, adapting and adjusting to whatever circumstance we find ourselves in. We learn to be content in good times as well as hard times. It is an attitude. When our focus is mainly on material things, we simply just want it and it's not a need.

Temptation cause us to compromise our principles to get what we think will make us happy. It is resulting in our appetite dictating to our morals and values rather than the other way around. We are led away from God and His way of doing things. Indeed, it is hard to be content in difficult times, but in searching for contentment, we draw closer to God in searching for the answers and fulfillment that we need to get through the rough times and seasons. Therefore, a content state or contentment is produced.

Have Content (Containment)

We grow into the spiritual place of containing the character and integrity of God. We possess or are the containers of the greatest treasure, The Holy Spirit and that nothing else matters other than having Christ. We recognize that we contain the Greater One and it lives on the inside. Therefore, we can face anything, go through any opposition and remain peaceful and joyful in any circumstances. Like Paul says, "*I can do all things through Christ who gives me the strength.*" (Philippians 4:13) We are filled with His Grace. It protects and covers us. We become containers for others who need to grow and develop spiritually. Keep in mind, there is always someone watching you, either to emulate, admire or they hate and want to destroy you. Their eyes are on you to see if you are really who you say you are or you possess or contain what you say you do. Others rely on us because they have seen what we have been through and endured. Our witness shows them that they too can be content knowing that God is in charge and that He oversees whatever goes on in their lives.

Therefore, realizing that the Holy Spirit that lives in every believer is in them also; and was placed there for equipping us to do whatever is vitally needed. Instead of complaining and moaning about what would and could be different, realize that you are equipped by the Holy Spirit. You can do all things through Christ that gives you the strength. (Phil. 4:13) What you are not able to do in your strength; God has assigned angels to work for you. You can now rest in God's peace, because you have angels waiting to receive their command.

Give Your Angels Their Job

Unemployment affects people both physically and spiritually. When we can't work and earn a paycheck to take care of ourselves and family, it causes people to be in a state of unrest. There are many Americans physically out of work and have been for many years. Just like there are many people that are unemployed, so are angels.

Many believers are unaware that they have angels

assigned to them to perform the jobs they can't do. They have angels that are waiting to be employed by them. Angels are waiting for you to give them daily assignments. Many believers have been taught erroneously and think that they are supposed to worship them. Instead, believers are worn out physically, mentally, emotionally and financially because they try to use only their own muscle and strength to produce the things they need to accomplish in life, instead of relying on their angel.

The truth is that Jesus is the final personal revelation of God and as such, he is the only one worthy of our complete faith, confidence, loyalty and service. Jesus is superior to angels and is God's anointed Messiah. This means Jesus is the only Savior. He is to be worshiped and Him only. We can not turn to or rely on no other. We may not compare or substitute Jesus to angels, to Moses, to the Levitical priesthood or any other sacrifices. God specifically assigned angels to minister to man.

The people of God are working hard trying to do spiritual battling that only angels are equipped to fight. Hebrews 1:14 says angels are "ministering" spirits sent to minister to the heir of salvation. Once again, angels are simply waiting for the believer to give them their command! They are waiting anxiously to fight on your behalf! Many in the Body of Christ simply do not understand their authority or angel's position. Instead angels stand guard waiting for us to tell them what to do.

The Bible describes angels as powerful spiritual beings that God created to perform specific jobs both in Heaven and on Earth. They help believers in their lives of serving God by making interference for us. The Bible mentions "hosts" of angels, but only name a few. Gabriel is the most mentioned, as a messenger to impart wisdom. Michael is the warrior that battles with the fallen angels. He battles those who sinned against God and became demons and fought for God's people. There is also Lucifer, the fallen angel who rebelled against God and was thrown out of heaven, along with those who followed him.

When we pray, we can command the angels assigned to our life to go into battle for us. There are many things that we cannot do, but when we give our angel the job of taking care of and handling assignments that are too difficult for us to handle, they will. Many people lack understanding about angels, therefore, many of them are walking around unemployed. They need a job! They want to fight, work, and get your stuff for you! In fact, some angels are sitting around with simply nothing to do because we simply don't know that we are to give them commands. We are to tell them what we need done. We are to give them a job! When we learn to give our angels their assignments, we no longer have to waste our energy, worry and lose sleep. We can be content knowing that God gave us His rest a long time ago. The things that are extremely difficult for us to do, angels were made to accomplish. Instead, we spend a lot of time worrying about how things are going to get done. You don't have to work overtime to make something happen. Neither do you have to spend sleepless nights worrying. You can sleep at night knowing that while you sleep, angels are working on your behalf.

The Power of Sleep

Lack of sleep is one enemy that keeps us from the rest that God has promised. Sleep is the healing agent that our body, soul and spirit need to live a peaceful life. Spiritual experts believe that dreams are one way that God speaks to his people. Every human being has dreams. Dreams are the language God uses prophetically. Whatever the dream, bad or good, it comes from God. "*In a dream, a vision of the night, When sound sleep falls on men, While they slumber in their beds, 16 Then He opens the ears of men, And seals their instruction.*" (Job 33:15-16) Since sleep is such a significant part of the human body, it is no surprise that Job and many Biblical writers mention it frequently. There are various reasons that many people have difficulty sleeping. Worry and stress are some of the reasons.

The word *sleep* is used literally to describe the state of the body in normal, unconscious repose. The most important stage is deep or REM sleep that occurs during the first two cycles. This cycle usually happens at the beginning of daybreak. REM (Rapid Eye Movement) sleep is the 5th stage of a good sleep pattern and usually occurs approximately 60 to 90 minutes after we first fall asleep. It is when we are in REM sleep that we dream. During this phase of sleep we experience something referred to as muscle atonia which basically means that our arms and legs become paralyzed. Some research on sleep says this prevents us from acting out the physical motions of our dreams. REM sleep improves memory because the areas of our brain that control the functions of learning and memory become stimulated. Could it be that many believers cannot hear and receive instructions from God, necessary to receive His rest, because we are not entering REM sleep?

Deep or REM sleep is also important in helping to renew and restore our energy. Sleep recharges our body's batteries, but in order to maximize the amount of charge we get, we need to have a full night's sleep. Sleep specialists say nine hours is the amount of sleep recommended. They believe this amount gives our body sufficient time to go through all of the stages of sleep as many times as needed. Lack of good restorative sleep is bad for our health. During stages 1 to 4 of non-REM sleep our heartbeat slows and our blood pressure drops by 10% on average. In sleep labs, it has been found that the hypothalamus secretes hormones such as dopamine that stimulate sleep and in later stages serotonin that bring deep sleep. Some experts believe lack of REM sleep deprives us of the rest needed to avoid significant risk of heart attack and stroke. Could it be that many of the health issues that believers are experiencing are because they are not entering the REM sleep?

You can see why REM sleep is important for both spiritual and physical reasons. In fact, it is crucial to a healthy life. The more REM sleep we experience in one night's sleep, the sharper our memories become, the more energized we will feel and the better our overall health becomes. Many of us try to sleep as little as possible. There are so many things that seem more interesting or important than getting a few more hours of sleep, but just as exercise and nutrition are essential for optimal health and happiness, so is REM sleep. The quality of your sleep directly affects whether you receive the instruction from God that is needed for a better and healthier quality of life. So could it be that when we go to bed, if we ask God to help us to relax, take away the cares of the world from our mind, we can enter into REM sleep and we can enter in God's rest. No other life activity can deliver so many benefits with so little effort!

Blessed Assurance

We must understand problems are only problems if we don't have solutions for them. In other words, we must go through the problem, to get the experience or become an expert and be able to produce solutions. Many experts say necessity is the mother of invention. There are many ways God equips us to discover solutions to problems, but often times we have accidentally run across solutions.

What we have to realize is Satan is strategic, but God does not need a strategy. God doesn't have to plan anything. Has it ever occurred to you that God is sure of everything? He doesn't have to stumble or come up with a solution by accident. He is confident and assured of everything. He is The Blessed Assurance! We are supposed to have this same assurance and the same contentment as it relates to being assured. When things come at us and bounce off, it is only because of the resolve and the resistance that is on the inside. This resistance is our ability to stay set and planted in the midst of everything that's going on around us.

The Holy Spirit in each believer equips us with the spirit of resistance. It allows us to stay mobile and stable. It prepares and equips us to have the answers and the solutions for any problem and issue that comes at us. We can therefore, be ready to provide the answer for whatever question or occurrence. We don't have to assume or guess; we can be confident and assured in our answers and solutions.

A spiritually renewed mind is, therefore, the most powerful component needed in trusting God to assist with any problems or unresolved issues. Whether we are asking God for spiritual, physical or financial help, we have to believe that even during our moments of feeling weak and it seems like we are losing the battle, our renewed and transformed mind has already won. Even before there is a physical manifestation, our belief must be that we have already received what we were asking and believing God for.

The body is the physical battlefield but our spirit does warfare that's invisible. We cannot see in the natural the war being waged. Therefore, the body will always be under attack. The more things we overcome, the fewer things can come at us, the more new obstacles the devil has to create. We do know that nothing under the sun is new; but the more knowledge and understanding we have, the more equipped we become and the less obstacles can defeat us.

Part Three

The Cure

The Cure

What is the true meaning of the word "cure"? Merriam-Webster Dictionary's definition is: "a drug, treatment, regimen, or other agency that cures a disease; recovery from a disease." On the other hand, Dictionary.com definition of cure is: "a means of healing or restoring to health; remedy." Cure means to bring relief to a person or animal of the symptoms of a disease or condition. The Word of God's meaning of remedy and cure is God heals and He is the Great Physician. He can heal any and everything. Little do many people know, reading His Word, is the remedy or cure for any sickness, disease, lack and poverty. The cure from sickness, disease and death itself, is His Rest.

Hebrews 4:9 reminds us, *"So there is a special rest still waiting for the people of God."* The remedy or cure is entering God's rest. For all who have entered into God's rest have rested from their labors, just as God did after creating the world. Sickness, disease, lack and poverty are not in His Rest. His peace, joy and tranquility are in His Rest. So let us do our best to enter that rest. If we have disobeyed God, as the people of Israel did, we will fall.

Chapter Five

Moving Forward Into His Rest

The Word of God encourages us to always move forward; "*So God set another time for entering His rest, and that time is today. God announced this through David much later in the words already quoted, "Today when you hear his voice, don't harden your hearts.*" (Hebrews 4:7) We can make it even through difficulties if we learn to "*press forward toward the mark of our high calling; which is in Christ Jesus*". (Philippians 3:14) When we reach for Him, even through the hard and most difficult times of our lives, God develops us through our most excruciating valleys and pitfalls.

The Word of God has a cleansing effect. It's like women during childbirth. She is uncomfortable during the entire nine months of pregnancy. Labor is usually the most difficult time during pregnancy; that's the time when she experiences the most pain. Pushing through the pain can be the most difficult thing. In order to bring the child into the world, she must push her new baby out. After the baby's arrival, she usually rests.

God allows pain because He wants to see how we handle and endure pain, while always moving forward to our next place. We are not to become stagnant and stuck in a place that's desolate, dry and unproductive. A spiritual reality is that we will always and forever experience spiritual seasons while we live on earth. Like the farmer, we too have responsibilities during their seasons as farmers. Just as farmers can discern the time of the natural seasons, we too can discern the spiritual season. There is a direct link between properly discerning the times and hearing God's lead in moving us forward from season to season.

"That'll Do" Spirit

Pain teaches us to excel. God has given each of His children a spirit of excellence. He works on us to perfect us into becoming the best we can be. Unfortunately, some of us have a "that'll do" spirit. "That'll do" spirit will cause us to miss God and prevent us from moving to bigger and greater things in life. What keeps many of us from attaining excellence is being lazy. We do not want to take the extra step and walk the extra mile that's needed to excel.

Another thing we must be cautious of is, expecting people to do and be what we think they should be or do. Often we judge folks unknowingly thinking and expecting they should be doing what we are doing and accomplishing what we can accomplish. It's important to always keep in mind, everybody didn't come from where we came, nor do they have our drive, our dedication or our determination. God does expect His people to be excellent, but He doesn't need us to condemn and judge others to force them into that excellence. The Holy Spirit can and will guide every individual to that place.

Many of us have a problem understanding God will bless us when we bless others. God wants to pay us for intangible things; things others cannot pay us for. God does not give rewards for the bare minimum of what we are asked to do or give. He wants us to go the extra mile and take the extra step. The difference between greatness and mediocrity is the extra effort we apply.

Can I Get A Witness?

Anyone that knows me, know that I am a giver and I love giving! For instance, the people closest in my circle always think and believe I give too much. If we read Psalm 112, that's who I am; I disperse and give. I thank God for that spirit of giving; I love it and the enemy hates me because I simply love people; all people. The Bible says, *"But I have prayed for you, that your faith fail not: and when you are converted, strengthen your brothers."* (Luke 22:32).

One of the biggest problems in the Black church or any church is people in the church have picks and cliques; they choose who they like. The Bible is filled with God admonishing us to not only love one another; but we must be diligent in showing that love, and not keep it hidden. We do understand showing everyone love does not mean everybody will hang out with us; but we must show people the same kind of love and affection. We can't pick and choose between people. When we do this, we form little cliques and acceptance club that cause strife and divide the church body.

Another enemy is that as believers, we should always pray for one another, but fail to do so. For example, one of our church members may be out sick. We should pray for them and others. Don't ever be so selfish, always thinking only about me and mine, that we don't pray for others around us; especially in the household of faith. This is one of God's tests just to see if we will be obedient.

What *Another* Test?

Recently, I was home alone doing absolutely nothing. I didn't realize it was another one of God's test. Sometimes you are tested and don't even realize it. Actually, I was simply bored! The problem with being bored is we can probably find something to do. God asks us the question, "Are you cool with being bored?" He asks this question because we can get antsy and start thinking about people and things that we should not think about. God wants to see if we can be patient and remain still even when our flesh is tempting us to do something we shouldn't do in our state of boredom. What happens when we are bored and can't find something constructive to do? The thought or person which comes to mind during our state of boredom may have an attachment to it on the other side when we are no longer bored. During the test, God may be trying to get us to a place of contentment until He blesses us with what He wants us to have, rather than settling for a spur of the moment or a "that will do for right now" blessing! God's Word exhorts us to *Wait on the LORD: be of good courage, and he shall strengthen thine heart: wait, I say, on the LORD."* (Psalm 27:14) Ultimately, during these tests, God is asking the question, "Can you rest"?

Be Anxious for Nothing, REST

Some of us have a problem with resting. The people in Hebrews were experiencing the same issue. They too didn't know how to rest. We know how to be "under arrest" but have a problem resting. Unfortunately with being under arrest, we don't have any choice about being still. The law controls what we can and cannot do. How do we rest when we can do other things? We have this restlessness or anxiousness about us which causes us to reach after things because we don't want to be lonely. We struggle with being by ourselves. God does require us

81

to be alone sometimes. It is during our alone time God can give us the peace and rest we need. God separates men and women of God, especially apostles, so we can be by ourselves; this allows God to speak to us so we can get things done.

One of the qualifiers in preparation for effective ministry is our ability to be separate or set apart. This separation allows an apostle or any of God's children to function properly. This period of separation allows God to speak to us because we are not busy doing everything else. An apostle cannot properly operate in the gift if his time of separation does not occur. It is vital for the apostle and other five-fold ministry gifts to allow this separation time. The Holy Spirit gives gifts as He wills, including the five-fold ministry gifts. There is a five step qualification process that tames and keeps us grounded to defeat loneliness and anxiousness when those feeling surface. It's the times of separation, suffering, serving, being sent, and son-ship that qualifies the men and women of God to operate properly, while we wait on God and His timing.

Could You Not Last One Hour with Me?
Crucifixion Time

One reason the Black church doesn't accomplish as much as it should is because we don't spend enough time by ourselves. We must come to understand that time alone is not isolation; it's gestation. Those are the times we must be in a position to hear and handle what God is revealing to us about ourselves and our purpose. There are some things God needs to reveal to us when we are by ourselves with Him. We are not spotless. Many of our issues are intimate, nasty and ugly; therefore we don't want others to know what He says to us. Though we may be aware of our issues, it's when we are alone that God works on the issues. He works it up, so He can work on it, and He can work it out! Some of our issues must be exposed and brought to the surface in order to be worked on. When we avoid time alone, we won't look our issues in the face and allow God to deal with them.

The problem is many people get into unhealthy relationships because they run from opportunities to be alone. We avoid being alone by seeking out family and friends to always occupy our time and space. Actually, God wants to put us in a place where our friends go to sleep, just as it happened to Jesus in His last few hours before His crucifixion. He asked His disciples, "*So, you men could not keep watch with Me for one hour.*"(Matthew 26:40) God need our friends to go to sleep so we can enter a place where there is a decision that needs to be made about our future. God needs our friends to go to sleep because we depend too much on other ways besides God to answer many of our needs. Sometimes friends can be the distraction from isolating ourselves and experiencing our crucifixion encounter. When we understand the real truth about God and His expectations of us, we will allow ourselves to be drawn us to Him to get the desired results needed to transform us into what He has called and chosen for us.

The church raves about the Golgotha experience, but Gethsemane was more painful than Golgotha. Gethsemane is where we make a choice; Gethsemane is where we are alone. It's the place when our friends have gone to sleep and have been narrowed down from twelve, four, to three. We have now gone from the multitude to the seventy, to the twelve and down to three. Eventually, we are alone; it is me and God. It is during these alone times that God asks a question. He has put us into situations that seems like we lack the strength to get through it. Despite knowing God is with us, we still ask God questions. We hope He would do whatever He needs to do, but hope He considers another way or method.

Can I Get A Witness?

Have any of us ever questioned God? Have any of us ever gone through something so painful, stressful and powerful that we almost wish God would use someone else or that He would use another way or method? Don't we sometimes wish God would use a doctor's method of giving pain killers, such as Novocain to numb or deaden the pain? Do we sometimes wish God could use anesthesia to put us to sleep so when we wake up, we already have the results needed to fix the pain or malfunction? Isn't it something that God allows us to stay awake and we have to feel and experience all that the pain?

No Pain No Gain

We are encouraged to know God could not have deadened our pain when He began to work on us. We can look at His example. When they tried to put vinegar in His mouth while He was hanging on the Cross; He turned His head away from the vinegar which was intended to be His analgesic to deaden the pain. We must feel the pain of being taken advantage of, from divorce and rejection, poverty, lack of money, making ends meet, being dealt with wrong, heartache, suffering, sickness and disease, and being back-stabbed by someone who we thought would never turn their back on us. Some of the hell that we have gone through was necessary because God wanted to know, 'Can I still get praise out of them through their pain'?

It's about entering a place of rest. We don't get there because we dream about rest; rather we get there through the obstacles we face. God wants to know if we can still remain calm in the midst of all our madness. He want to know that while folks are still so burdened and heavy laden by their problems and issues, 'Can He really still get a good praise from us"? God says, "Even when we go to church mad and sad, we ought to praise Him!" While feeling rejected, we ought to praise God! All God is asking is that, "Can they bless Me at all times"? He says, "I know what the symptoms and diagnosis says; but can they bless Me in spite of'? A true worshipper and a true praiser is someone who will worship and praise regardless of what is going on in their life. They know they still owe God praise. They not only know they owe Him praise, they continually give Him the praises due to Him, in spite of.

Resting is Not Laziness

Entering into a place of rest is not a place of laziness. To get to the place of rest, we cannot be lazy. Don't get it twisted. Resting is living in a peaceful state. It's confidently enjoying life while waiting for God's promises to become reality. it does not mean lacking responsibility and accountability for our life. It does not mean sitting around in a fantasy, anticipating that blessings will fall from the sky and hit us on the head. Resting is not fooling us from taking responsibility for our desires, dreams, and vision. Resting is to know God has already made all of the provisions needed to bring forth the blessings in our lives. The rest is, while waiting, we put our trust and faith in Him.

We should ask ourselves, am I lazy or do I have rest? We will know if we are lazy or not. If we are not lazy, lazy people won't be bothered with us. Some people aren't willing to do what it took us to do to enter into the rest. Lazy people don't go the extra mile in helping others. We know that we are not lazy if we pick up someone who is in need of a ride or we give gas money to someone in need. Going the extra mile is going out of our way in helping and blessing others, Have we ever blessed people? There's a saying, "The hand that you feed will end up biting you." If that's true, that's cool. Just keep right on blessing others, anyway!. God will bless us for whatever we do to make something happen for someone else. I would rather be in the position to give, and have it to give, than to be in the position of needing the help. Either God will lay someone at our gate or we will be laid at someone else's gate. Which would you prefer?

Has someone been laid at your gate? Or are you lying at someone else's gate?

Whether we are givers or receivers, there is a rest for the people of God. It doesn't mean we have to die to receive it. Some of us are waiting to die, but that's not what He is talking about. We will be alive to enjoy the rest. The Scriptures in Genesis 2:2, when God dealt with rest, He is dealing with promise. He deals with the Promised Land. When God was finished building in Genesis, He said it was good. He then laid back and enjoyed His rest. He is saying the same thing to us. It is time for us to rest! That doesn't mean living a dwindling life. What He means is living in a more abundant life, a healthy life free from lack and poverty, sickness and disease.

Some of us deserve more than what we have right now. But we have to want better and it's coming if we don't complain or settle. Never settle for what we have in the present. Keep trusting for what He will bless us with in the future. Always dream for something greater; dream for something more. Keep believing God has more for us. Have you ever dreamed of better things, a bigger space, more money, or better health? That means God has given you a sneak preview of your future. Dream Baby, Dream!

Who's in the Boat?

Here is where God is about to take us. We find ourselves in Mark chapter four. This particular passage of Scripture tells the story of and deals with moving forward but running into storms, problems and difficulties. Why would God give instructions that cause our surroundings to get worse? Here is the familiar story of Jesus calming the seas. We find Mark 4:35, says *"And the same day, when the even was come, he saith unto them, Let us pass over unto the other side."* In other words Jesus said; let us begin moving from where we are. We have been here long enough. I have been in this stage too long!.

How many times do we get so comfortable in a place that is uncomfortable? How many times have we settled because we knew it may take more energy to move on? We have to be people so radical for God that nothing else matters; we go for broke. Another problem that some of us have is that we allow our personality to outweigh our purpose. God has given each of us individual personalities, but our purpose should overshadow our personality. God created us to be purpose-led, not purpose-driven. Therefore our churches should be purpose-led churches, not purpose-driven.

We need to analyze ourselves and where we are and decide if we are ready to move forward. In this

Scripture, Jesus was saying we need to go somewhere else. Have you ever been around people and they are the same way all the time? It would be easy to profile them. We have been around them so long we can tell how long they will be sad and mad; and how long they will be looking at us the right way and all of a sudden they will flip on us! Have you ever been around people who have a personality disorder called flipology and tripology?

Stop Tripping

Actually, flipology and tripology are words the Holy Ghost dropped in my spirit. The spiritual definition is when people flip and trip on you in the blink of an eye. The spiritual personality disorders causes' negative behavior that is so unpredictable. The disorders cause mood swing. They think they are normal. The behavior occurs because of an uncertainty of who they are and the lack confidence in themselves. Their behavior and reaction toward others really has nothing to do with the other person(s). Caution: Do not take it personally! It is the feeling of insecurity with which they struggle. What actually happens is that they are in a spiritual battle with the enemy within them. The battle they are engaging in causes them to retaliate toward others. These behaviors fluctuate and they are very unpredictable. On the other hand, we are completely clueless to the reasons for the negative behavior toward others.

Unfortunately, the display of these personality disorders reveals the unrest in these individuals. Healing and deliverance only comes through prayer, confessing and admitting to God that we want to be delivered from it. Pretending the problem doesn't exist and blaming others for it, will not heal these personality disorders. Until these disorders are dealt with, our emotions will be like a roller coaster ride; full of drama. We will not have God's peace that is needed to live a restful life.

Can I Get A Witness?

The sad reality is that I know someone who was exhibiting the behavior and they had the nerve to justify it by telling me, "This is how I am. This was how I was born." I responded, "Well you need to get born again!"

You Must Be Born Again!

When we get born again, how we were born, gets trampled out! Imagine how many un-born again-people are walking around with a Bible up under their arm? WOW! They have a church title in the church! Scary, isn't it? What's ironic is they are in the church and mistreat people. They have not been reborn. Many may not agree with what I am about to say, but I am under the impression that getting saved is not necessarily being born again. Being Holy Ghost-filled is being born again. We have a lot of saved people who are not born again. Think about this. How can we have the Holy Ghost when there has been no crucifixion? Regular church attendance does not mean we are Holy Ghost-filled. It does mean we are saved. "Saved" simply means a confession or a belief, but Holy Ghost-filled is a born again experience and transference of the mind.

When we are Holy Ghost-filled, it simply means being chosen; versus being saved means we are called. For those who don't know, "Holy Ghost" is the same as "Holy Spirit." Holy Ghost is used more frequently by older saints of God. We hear Holy Spirit more often today. We need to understand many of us don't want to go through the death experience. When the Bible starts talking about terrestrial, it means territorial, dirt, laying axe to the root, and being rooted and grounded.

Can I Get A Witness?

God said, "Sammy, you have been missing it for so long." I said, "What do you mean God"? God said, "The first place of ground that I am talking about is you." He said, "Why are you trying to conquer other ground, why are you trying to take other ground, why are you trying to take territory, why are you trying to enlarge your church when your own personal territory is still being terrorized by spirits that you have not conquered yet?" God said, "How dare you try to clean up someone else's dirt and your own dirt has not been dealt with yet"? Sweep around your own front door.

We have got to recognize and understand something is wrong with us before we can expose someone else's issues. It's our own problem, when we can't deal with someone else's problem. Both Mark and Luke are in agreement. We too, need to move on to the other side. We need to move from our current condition before we can enter into God's rest. We must take a look in the mirror; acknowledge the truth about ourselves and surrendering our heart to the Holy Spirit.

Be Steadfast, Not Stuck

The people of God are reminded that they are to always be steadfast, immovable, abounding in the work. And it reminds us that when we do, their labor is not in vain. (1 Corinthians 15:58). Blessed are those who remain steadfast under trial, for when he has stood the test, he will receive the crown of life. (James 1:12). On the other hand, let us not confuse steadfast with becoming stuck. When we talk about steadfast, it is like a double sword when it pertains to how and when we apply it. Let us be sure not to use operating in a steadfast position to accomplish our personal agenda. Often times, people say they are being steadfast, when actually they are operating in disobedience. They don't want to submit to an area that needs submission, therefore they say that they are operating in steadfastness. When they operate for the convenience of accomplishing their own agenda it is called being "stuck". According to God's agenda, steadfastness is from the quality of one of the spiritual gifts that God gave to men. We are to operate in it because God have placed in His people the strength and stamina to be planted and become like trees planted by the rivers of water. He wants us to exhibit the strength and elasticity of a palm tree. Anchored that even through the fierce wind, storm or opposition, we bounce back in position. Refusing to bend and buckle under the uncertainties and pressures of life. The Hebrews belief system was so lifeless, but yet they refused to give it up. They didn't realize that accepting and embracing the new power would give them the power to sustain and be like the palm tree.

Conclusion

Most of our lives we were taught that we have to die to go to our eternal place to get rest, but that's not true. "*You Don't Have To Be Dead To Rest In Peace*"! We are living in a fast, uncertain and changing world. We don't know from one day to the next what changes, problems or issues will be. The world is forever evolving, but so is God. But in spite of all that goes on around us from day to day, our hope and faith must be in Jesus Christ. As long as you don't give up hope, believe and receive His Word that no matter what is taking place around us, He will never leave or forsake us, and we can enter in to His Rest.

Many of God's people are confused, discouraged, have lost hope and are spiritually dead! There are some that are jobless and living in lack and poverty. Many have sickness and disease and walking around in critical condition. Others are on a gurney, being transported to the morgue. Some are at their funeral waiting to bury, but the resurrecting power that brought Jesus from the grave lives in you! Whatever your condition is, this book was written to pull you out of your grave and give new life. The fact that you are at the end of this book could be God confirming that He heard your prayers, see your condition, showed up through this book to introduce you to the cure and answer you need to have a peaceful, restful, and abundant life.

Are you tired of the problems and issues of your uncomfortable seasons in your life, dictating and have convinced you of how you feel? You can go through your problems and stay in control of the stresses that cause you not to be in peace and enjoy your life. The peace and rest of God can become a lifestyle for you. Now that you have read this great resource, it is time to enter into His rest. The Bible declares in (Hebrews 4:9-11) *"So there is a special rest still waiting for the people of God. For all who have entered into God's rest have rested from their labors, just as God did after creating the world. So let us do our best to enter that rest..."*

My hope and prayers is that you embrace your wilderness, take God's Word and apply the principles you have read. Learn and mix it with your faith, so you can live a stress-free life. You *can* enjoy your life! *You Don't Have to Be Dead To Rest In Peace!*

References/Credits

The Living Bible 1971 Edition

Thomas Nelson Holy Bible KJV

Merriam-Webster Dictionary

Physicians Desk Reference Book/ Pdw.com

The New International Webster's Standard Dictionary (2006)

Thorndike-Barnhart Student Dictionary (updated edition)

cdc.gov/nchs/data/hus/hus09_InBrief_MedicalTech

Strong's Exhaustive Bible Concordance

Thomas Kincade Holy Bible

Jordana Adkins, *Healthy Lifestyle: Ultimate Tips for Healthy Living - How to Easily Maintain a Healthy Lifestyle in Your Busy and Stressful Everyday Life*

The Art of Peaceful Living by Allan Lokos (Jan 5, 2012)

Principles of Addiction Medicine by American Soc. of Addiction Medicine - Magazine Column/ Apr.2013 BibleGateway.com:

New King James Version (NKJV) - Bible

http://www.abibleconcordance.com/Contents.html

http://www.mayoclinic.org/diseases-conditions/high-blood-cholesterol/in-depth/statin-side-effects/

www.helpguide.org/mental/stress_signs.htm

www.webmd.com/balance/stress.../effects-of-stress-on-your-bod...

www.insight.org/resources/bible/hebrews.html

http://www.journals.elsevier.com/artificial-intelligence/

www.kingjamesbibleonline.org/

www.biblestudytools.com/kjv/

About the Author

Apostle Sammy C. Smith is Founder and Presiding Bishop of Grace Cathedral Christian Fellowship, Inc. His ministry began over thirty years ago from a small Shaw Air Force Base Chapel, to the building of Grace Cathedral Ministries, Sumter S.C, and currently the planting and transitioning of Grace Cathedral Ministries in Greenville, South Carolina.

He is an author, conference speaker, preacher, and teacher. He has conducted revivals and seminars throughout the country. His unique preaching and teaching ministry brings revelation to the Body of Christ under a prophetic anointing.

Apostle Smith strongly believes that "if Jesus is lifted up, HE will draw all man unto Him." God has now enlarged his territory through published spiritual growth and development publications that is changing the lives of God's people. This book is his first published book and upcoming projects are on the way.

He lives by, "If God be for us, who can be against us".

For more information concerning the Apostolic Ministry of Apostle Sammy C. Smith and a listing of available books, publications and CD messages, you may email, twitter, Instagram, call, or write:

Grace Us Living Publications

Email: graceusliving@yahoo.com
Website: graceusliving.com
Phone: 843-406-3499

Grace Cathedral Ministries
612 Poinsett Highway
P.O. Box 5719
Greenville, SC 29606
Phone: (864)241-3101
grace@gracecathedralministries.org

NOTES

<u>NOTES</u>